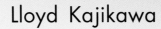

Lloyd Kajikawa

Contents

Rigby

A Harcourt Achieve Imprint

www.Rigby.com
1-800-531-5015

A desert is a place with very little water.
It doesn't rain often in the desert.
This makes the desert a very dry place.

The bright sun shines down on the desert almost every day. That's why days are very hot in the desert.

3

Plants need water to live.

A desert doesn't have much water,

but some plants can live in a desert.

How do they do it?

Some plants keep
water inside.
This cactus is one
of those plants.
This is
a saguaro cactus.

Saguaros can keep water
inside for a long time.
Saguaros are able
to grow wider
to make room
for the water.
This helps
saguaros
grow big
and strong.

Some saguaros
can grow to be
50 feet tall!

Animals in the desert
need food and water.
Some animals find
food and water
in the saguaros.

This woodpecker makes holes in the saguaro, looking for food and water.

Some animals look for places
where they can hide from the sun.
This snake stays under a rock all day
and only comes out at night.

Other animals like this roadrunner
stay in the sun a lot.
Roadrunners love to run through the desert.

Many animals eat
the fruit and the seeds
of the saguaro.
They also drink
the saguaro's juice.
These owls make
their homes in saguaros.

14

Saguaros are
good places
for animals
to live in the desert.

Index